Silent Whispers

Also by Samantha Jo Gabardi:
The Heart Speaks,
Whispers of a Silent Heart,
& Dear Heart.

Silent Whispers
a collection of poetry and prose
by Samantha Jo Gabardi

Independently Published
United States

Copyright © by Samantha Jo Gabardi

All rights reserved.
No part of this book may be reproduced in any form or by any electronic or mechanical means including information storage and retrieval systems, without permission in writing from the author. The only exception is for instances of cited quotations and book reviews or articles written about the book and/or author.

ISBN-9798743982608

First Printing August 2021
Independently Published
Cover design by Debbie Hainey

Printed in The United States of America

I have spent the whole of my life giving love away to others. I never really thought of giving any to myself..

I don't have walls around my heart anymore, I have doors, that you may enter and exit as you please. It makes for a much easier way to get into my heart, and out. If you're there, I will simply take care of all that is you; and if you are set on leaving, exit as you please. I will still love you nonetheless.

The more I understand,
the quieter I become.

Our souls will always ache when we're not where we're meant to be.

Aren't we all just dying to live and find life?

Sometimes, we open up
the novel of our life,
allowing people to read
our pages, just to watch
them burn the book in
the end, and that's okay.
That's perfectly okay
because we can always
write a new one.

How is it that my
soul can be so in love
with words and yet,
not trust them?

Sometimes I wonder if losing one's mind is the only proper way to discover it?

The sufferings of life become so much easier when you're holding my hand and heart.

And he always loved me sweeter than the aching in my throat.

A love that is lasting
is one that chooses
you every single day.

Anything is a love language when two are in agreement.

Find someone who
can make every
piece of you ache but
always in the most
beautiful way.

It's the spaces between
the heartbeats that
always mean the most.

Maybe life is always supposed to be a tragedy? Perhaps we are here to embrace those sufferings so that we can find our wings?

As long as there is life, there is hope.

Laughter makes for better seconds, better sounds, and healthier bones.

When everything becomes nothing, nothing becomes everything.

Where you place
your importance,
you place your life.

It only hurts when it matters.
Everything matters.

I always had a
love for things
that never
loved me back.

Once you start thinking about not thinking about it, it starts all over again.

Beautiful heart, soft soul, untamable spirit, complexity of mind..

Me

But do they make you
feel seen, though?

I don't know
exactly what a
soulmate is,
but I do know
that it feels
much like you.

Forever dreaming
of getting lost in
the forest and you.

You're ready for everything, but you believe nothing.

We must be cautious of the thoughts we entertain, for like the blowing of hot air into a balloon, that which we breathe life into will expand.

Anxiety used to be
a heavy weight I
hauled around,
but when I sat
with it and
listened awhile, I
found wisdom,
life, and ultimately
freedom.

Beautiful isn't the flower that is standing so very high; it is the one that is trampled underfoot and yet, still reaches for the sky. 🌻

Brave, beautiful, you.

I always hang on to those things that I love with both hands, never really learning how to let go, because I was taught about forever by those that we're always saying goodbye.

There's always so much more to give, but people don't know how to receive it, and so we waste away alone.

There was chaos
living inside of her, a
beautiful fucking
dream that could raise
even the demons from
off their knees.

Let us not get so obsessed with the past and caught up in the future that we forget the actual moment is now.

Surround yourself with people who bring laughter to your soul. It tends to make life a lot lighter.

How someone treats
you will always be how
they feel about you.
Listen to what they do
and take what is said
with a grain of salt.

"We'll find a way," love whispered.

Not everyone who asks how you are is genuinely interested in your well-being. Be very careful with whom you share your soul.

To win an argument,
one must become
Silent..

I don't know about anyone else, but I find my strength in loving, caring, and being tender with people and things. It fills my soul when she is weeping, and sorrow cannot hold on when a rush of joy comes flooding in.

This is your heart,
and if they aren't
willing to take
care of it, then
their love is a lie.

You better take care of her. You better scoop her up in your hands and hold her tighter than all her troubles because that woman is like water, and if you're not careful enough with her heart, she'll slip right through your fingertips. I can assure you that there is a man out there who has done the groundwork necessary for a relationship that is both willing and ready to take care of all that she is. Tread lightly, Sir, for souls such as hers are rare.

Genuine kindness is no ordinary act but a gift of rare beauty.

It's okay to cry, sweet one. It's perfectly acceptable because life is hard. Tears do not show weakness but strength of heart. They are an indication that one is in tune with one's soul, and that is a beautiful thing. Very rarely will you find a person that is brave enough to look within. So weep, sweet angel; cry it out and then lift your head and carry on once more. Brave, beautiful, you.

The strongest of wildflowers 🌻 bloom silently in the moonlight to the sound of darkness.

She gave away
so many
pieces of
herself that
she just
disappeared.

Learn to let go of the people who let go of you, but always hold on to the lessons.

There's nothing complicated about taking care of a person's heart. So if this seems to be a difficult task for you, you should probably step back and do some inner healing. Learn how to love yourself first so that you can offer that same tenderness to another soul. That is all.

Some relationships are like riding a teeter-totter: back and forth, up and down. Don't be afraid of jumping off the seesaw and letting their ass smack the ground.

If life hands you
an everlasting
soul, hold tight
because you won't
find many hearts
that exist like that
anymore.

Once I had tasted every tragedy known to man, I went out on a journey and discovered Pandora's Box. Cracking the lid back open, I found hope and pulled out just enough to allow myself the ability to carry on one more day.

It takes an incredible amount of strength to go through tragedies and still have the ability to look at the world, find goodness, smile, and offer tenderness to another.

Courage,
sweet one..

Sometimes, that's all we need, just a strong shoulder we can lay our heart upon until things become light again. That's all.

Kindness isn't just something you offer at your convenience. It is a way of life, something you should be consistent in every single day.

A wise friend once told me that when people are ugly, take all that love I would have offered them and give it to myself. Go out and do something for me that I enjoyed, and I did. My soul became lighter, and I was lifted from off my knees. I'll be forever thankful for that wisdom passed on to me from another heart that I hold dear, for it carried me when I hadn't any strength left of my own. They held me tighter than all my troubles with just their words of wisdom alone. I will always love and appreciate you, my sweet and dearest friend.
                For you, K.D.

The best of friends
will always teach
you just how to love
yourself.

My heart does choose
to love, for it has
silently borne witness
to many wonderful
and tragic things.

The trees hold so many of my untouched secrets.

Her soul doth sing a song that only the birds can understand.

I watched as she cried, and I don't mean lightly. She wept bitterly. So much so that oceans were created from her salty tears. I watched as she raged, not angrily, but with sorrow of heart, and I marveled at the fire that shot out from her nostrils and at her voice of thunder as it rocked my soul and violently shook the ground beneath me. And the only conclusion I could come to was that the sky, like me, had a soul and could feel, and she too was beautiful for it.

Here I sit in the land of magical things, where the sun rises on us all, and everyone is tender with one another.
My Hopeful Heart

I don't like subtle.
Come in, my love,
rip my heart wide
open and drown
in all that is me.

There was no turning back now; I was in too deep. I had fallen head over heart for his charm and the way he held my heart so tenderly.

And sometimes, he touched my heart with something as simple as a whisper.

What God has joined together,
let no man rip asunder.

Take my hand, darling, and lead me through the darkest corners of your mind. Show me all of the things that haunt you, and let me love you there.

But can't you see the way the moonlight twinkles on your skin? You are the entire midnight sky.

Get naked, strip yourself
bare down to the bone and
show me your darkness,
your vulnerabilities, all of
the things that broke you,
and I will show you how
there's still so very much of
you to be loved.

I went looking for a fairytale
and found one at the end of
each week as I finished off
yet another good book.

There comes a certain point in your life when you have to sit down and ask yourself some serious questions. Like, what's the point of having me in their life? What's their goal? Why do they want a relationship? Things like that. I know my only goal has ever been to build and grow a strong relationship, one that is full of kindness, love, respect, and taking care of another person, their heart, and all that is them. I seek for time, a lifetime of memories that can be tucked up under the ribs. Things that are lasting. If that's not what they're in it for, what's the point? As I said before, what's the goal? what purpose does it serve? What are they in it for? Love is not self-seeking, it always puts another before its own self. It is patient. It is kind. Love is easy. It is people that make it hard.

The window to the soul is not always the eyes; sometimes, it's the mouth. Be careful with whom you share your soul; not everyone you're speaking to is a friend.

Sometimes, they level up a little too late.

In all my years of searching, I have finally found the love of my life. She was gazing back at me from the mirror.

Don't get too caught up in pretty words. As beautiful as they are, and as much as you wish to cling to them, a person's actions will always tell all.

He did not fancy me much anymore, for I discovered my voice, and it spoke loud. It thundered across the sky, and his bones, they did tremble.

Resurrect not the past; she has nothing further to give.

And when I fall, I do so like a heavy rain that floods. I have the power to drown them all within my bones.

Always dancing a slow dance with my shadows. Spiraling even further down still into the depths that chain me.

Sometimes, my heart aches, and there's not much I can do with it save to just let it

BLEED

I think I'll run away
now, with all my
hopes and dreams. It
is high time I flee
with the only thing
left that's holding me.

I wonder how many
3 am drives down
dusty back roads it's
going to take before
this ghost of you
stops haunting me?

Hearts bleeding and
still yet beating for
another that they
might not have to taste
what it feels like when
the warmth of the
lifeblood turns cold.

But are they strong enough to hold your darkness, though?

And if you were kind to another today, you will have succeeded at this thing we call LIFE.

Meet me in that place where I grow tired of being strong and carry my wearied heart once more.

The stars aligned, our hearts collided, and all that made up us was consumed.

I could be given a thousand sunsets, a million and one midnight skies, and it wouldn't mean as much as one tender moment with you.

And it all fell into place so effortlessly.

A thousand people in the room, and the only one she's looking for is you.

The only place I long to be is right where you are.

Come, fall into me, rest your weary heart upon mine a while, and disappear from the weight of it all even if only for a moment. Come, my love.

All that I would ever ask of you, my love, is that you would allow me to hold you just a little bit tighter, for a little while longer, until all of the cracks sealed inside of your heart and your bones fell gently back into place.

If you love someone,
tell them because
time is fleeting, and
moments, they're lost
in the blink of an eye.

Sometimes, all you can do is breathe through the gut-wrenching chaos and hang on to hope with both hands because that's all that's left holding you.

It was beautiful the way she loved others, for when she cared for someone, she would be willing to yank the moon from the sky and change ocean tides just to see them smile, including the ones that hadn't the intentions of ever loving her back.

I am thankful for those who shit on me; it gives me something to write about.

I knew it. I knew when you were leaving that day for work; when you didn't even turn to kiss my face, I knew. Like the guy who goes after milk, never to be seen again; that's how it felt. I just knew it was the last goodbye I'd ever hear again. There was no I love you, no softness in your voice, just an aching sorrow as you simply said, "bye." I knew. I just wish you had left my heart at the door.

It takes a long time for a loyal one to get to the point of not caring, but once they reach that point, that's it because the pain has become unbearable, and they must now shield their own heart from the one who promised never to hurt it but breaks it at every turn.

It is in the dying that we find life, meaning, and the beauty in things.

I am who I am, not what you believe me to be.

Don't spend your life explaining yourself to people who will never see you. Let them have their opinions because I can assure you that there are some who have the ability to get outside of themselves long enough to try to understand and get to know you as a person. I know they're few and far between, but they do exist. Wait for them and continue on being the magical, beautiful soul that you are. I promise you, one day, someone will see you.

Some people have no business being in a relationship, but there they are, wreaking havoc on beautiful, innocent souls who had nothing but good intentions for them.

Love is not self. It will always live and breathe for others.

Go, light up the souls of many, breathe life even into your enemies. Heap those burning coals of fire upon their heads. Be so authentic in your kindness that when others speak ill of you, no one will believe it.

She is a wild wanderer, always fierce at heart, with a fire in her eyes and thunder in her bones, and always she rises higher just as the liliums do when the sun beats down upon her petals. Do not try to tame her, for you will not succeed but instead, run beside her, allowing her to show you how beautiful it is to be set free.

Come, my love, meet
me in that place
where you grow
tired of being strong,
and allow me to
carry your wearied
soul once more.
Come..

There is no shallow end in love. You have to be willing to drown.

Don't be lucky to have her, be deserving.

And when the love story comes, pray for your heart.

Infinite words,
and yet I still
struggle to
capture the
beauty of all that
makes up you.

There are these things that you do to me, so many things, beautiful and wonderful things that cannot be named, and I could get lost in that kind of feeling, well.. forever

Those eyes. I look at those eyes, glimmering rays of hope bright enough to light up the entire midnight sky, and I want to inch a little nearer and scoop you up with both hands, with my heart, and hold yours ever so tightly. I long for moments where I can breathe you in. Time, time, and time again, to trace your smile with my fingertips as you rest easy, your head on my heart, soaking in the silent spaces of your heartbeat for as long as life would allow. But for now, patiently, I wait for you to speak so that I may become intoxicated by the breath of your mouth, allowing those words to penetrate deep inside of my soul and unknowingly holding me through all of these moments until our moments become as one evermore.

I'm drawn to you, and for you, I'll wait. And even if we cannot touch in this life, one day we will meet face to face, even if it's on the other side of forever. Your soul, it calls to me, and I will wait.

His soul made mine ache. It was the beautiful kind of ache that one would wish never to go away. Stay..

There will come a day
when I will lay down my
pen, and my paper soul,
allowing the book to close
around me, watching as
the rest of the story so
beautifully writes itself.

Love will find you when you least expect it, where you do not seek, and in a place that you've never even dreamed. It will present itself when you are falling in love with yourself and with all that life has to offer. Love, well.. She will greet you with a kiss when you're not even paying attention at all.

I saw a shooting star tonight and did not think upon myself. No, my one and only wish was for you, that your wearied heart could find a place of peace and know what it was to rest in the arms of a genuine soul who cared.

Emerge from your chrysalis, sweet soul, rise from your slumber, for there is a life to be lived; your wings are now ready, and there's a journey to be had. 🦋

Go inward, and you will find your way out.

Stop taking advice from others; listen to your own soul, for she knows the way.

We're all wrong, but sometimes we get it right.

See, that's the thing with angels who were fashioned in Hell; they burn people, but never on purpose.

You can't break a broken heart; you can't. It's like salt; no matter how many times you crush it, always it keeps its shape and the things contained within, even when in pieces.

I'm in need of a thing, so many things that just don't exist in this realm.

Forever that girl who falls in love with the sky at sunset, the trees in Fall, and everything else when it is dying.

I wish to be as water now, that I may forever travel the Earth; that people could come to me when wearied hearts can no longer be carried and dip their toes into my soul, rippling an unending circle of love. May I be as water now, never apologizing for my tides and waves that do consume? I know I am too much of everything, for I run deep, but never for those who have the ability to swim.

Some of the most meaningful conversations I have ever experienced were the ones that took place in the stillness

WITH MYSELF..

Find a lyric full of life that embeds and goes round and round and chant it until it washes out the darkness. 🎶

♥
Music is a love language..

Anyone else look at the world and feel like an unwelcome stranger?

Truth is a narrow path, not often traveled.

Sometimes, the straw that breaks the camel's back is something as simple as the lack of a genuine soul that cares.

'Tis the woe that won't let go, not me, for I tied bows in my veins, and still you got to me.

Lost
in a world not my own.
Lost
and feeling the weight
all alone.
Lost
is sometimes the best place
to be because
Lost
is the exact place that I
found me.

Sorrow has always been a good friend to me, for she always holds my hand, showing me how things should be.

Silence is a response that I'm still trying to navigate.

Dreaming of a place where I can pick a bouquet of wildflowers that will never wilt, where kindness is King, and a home where the only law is

Love

This world, it moves far too fast for me; too in a hurry to get nowhere, it seems. So I shall step out of the race, far out of reach, sitting a while with stillness, enjoying every breath because it's necessary.. Most needed for peace, for sanity, for life, and feeling what is hidden between the silent spaces of this gift of a heartbeat. It is time for me to release everything, be still, and just breathe.

I grew weary and tired of breaking my ribs and piercing my heart, trying to fit myself into places not meant for me. This is not my home; I'm only passing through, and now I understand why I can't seem to fit anywhere. My place is in the stars, where the angels do sing, where I worship not others but the only ONE who has ever cared for enough for me to sit with my broken, catching my tears in a jar, strengthening me. And I will wait most patiently for that ONE to arrive, freeing me of this castle that keeps me caged, these stones that cut at me, and I will count it all joy that I was found worthy of that calling.

I woke up, and you were gone again today, just like yesterday and all the other days before, and I just wonder if I'll ever get used to your absence because I only know how to love, not let go. Pieces of me are made up of everyone I've ever encountered, and so, there is no letting go, only a moment to rebuild around you. Something new, the turning of the page, and a new chapter begins. I always win at losing, heart continuously taking a bruising. I'm lost, but only for a moment in time. I pick up my guitar, knocking the dust away; I play. Strumming through the chords once more, just like I used to, before.. you. And now, I will live, and I will breathe, for you can no longer steal my melody. Just an angel with broken wings, but always, I rise. There's nothing beautiful in saying goodbye; I tried. I fucking tried, I always do, but this one is on you, and to you, it was just a game; you win. Here's to all the befores that will never happen again; I wish you well, my friend.

I don't grieve quietly; torrents of waves wash over me. Tears like lifeblood coursing through my veins; even you will feel the pain.. Again and again, until the soul is cleansed, so hold on to what you have with both hands. Cling tight, for there's a storm a raging; this is what I call 'the uncaging'. There's nothing beautiful that comes when the souls of angels do cry, for this one's name is Tempest, and together we ride..

Sometimes, the straw that breaks the camel's back is something as simple as an unkind word. You never know what people are going through. Some are locked away behind closed doors with their mouths sewn shut just to keep the peace alive. So please, be careful with the words you lay on the backs of angels who never even meant any harm at all.

Hers was but a brave heart, always trying to remain tender, strong, and loving in a cold and bitter world.

In the end, it will be the love that saves us.

And then, she simply
walked away, and a trail
of stardust followed.

It ISN'T what it is; it's what you make of it.

Put your doubt up on
a shelf..

No, higher.

Maybe the stars
look down
when we shine
and make
wishes on us?

There's a lot of beauty in humanity; you just have to peel the layers back to find it.

The most courageous people I know are the ones who have had their hearts completely dismantled and torn to shreds, and there they are, even still, holding it carefully inside of their shaking hands, offering it over once more. Even in pieces, they're still willing to trust another. That is what I call beautiful. Brave, beautiful, you.

It wasn't until after all my insides had been torn out that I was able to remain completely open in my vulnerability, unafraid of what men could do unto me or the pain that possible could be. Fear lost its hold, and I was grateful.

Sometimes, life hands us gifts but not always in the way we think. Sometimes those blessings look much like pain, broken dreams, tattered hearts, and bruised souls. Growth is necessary for wisdom. Tis the key to all things. For had we not known pain, how could we ever experience the fullness of love? Love isn't just pretty things; it is made up of all things terrible and wonderful, and we cannot have one without the other. Be thankful.

I grabbed hold of
pain with both hands
and all of my heart,
allowing it to shake
my insides, ridding
me of the all that
was not meant to be
there, and I have
become beautiful for
it. I am thankful.

There is no harm that will come from my bones, for I know nothing more save how to love.

I have waited
lifetimes for you,
and I have the
patience in my
bones to wait for a
thousand and one
more.
I. Will. Wait.

You're still the only one I see in this crowded room, the only one I look for, and the one place I long to be.

Perhaps if I hold my breath, it will delay time long enough for me to remain forever lost in this moment with you?

There are women out there praying for a man with a heart like yours. Keep your head up, sweet one; your time will come soon enough.

Learn to love the pieces of you that people have scorned the most.

If you don't have a safe space to be open and honest with your partner, but they're yelling at you or giving the silent treatment instead, that's not a partnership; it's a prison.

Some of you women need to figure out how to be a lady and take care of your man. All too often, I see the souls of amazing men being tarnished and are now shut down because of selfish, self-seeking, ill-willed individuals who refuse to grow. Heal so that you don't ruin things for those of us who know how to be tender and treat them as they deserve. That is all.

Love requires sacrifice, but not of your morals, boundaries, or self-respect.

If it's not your goal to bring a smile to their face, you don't deserve them.

Do yourself a favor, get to know who a person is, not your idea of what you wish them to be.

You want to
vibe with me,
rise higher,
for I leveled
up eons ago.

The quality of your life is made up of those who surround you. Tend your garden most carefully, and weed out the ones who disrupt your soul.

She dressed for her heart, and her outfit appeared to be very much like it, as black as a starless night.

Just an angel with broken wings, but always I rise.

You won't break me of the kindness; you won't. My heart is stronger than iron, even in pieces. Even after all the chaos, there's still love tucked up under my ribs, enough to light up an entire midnight sky for a thousand and one generations. You'll see, you just can't break me.

I am not what happened to me; I am what I choose to become.

I don't have room in my life anymore for people who haven't matured enough to understand manners. If one wishes to disrespect me, they may do so from a distance, for I am worthy of being treated with kindness. That is all.

Headed for the horizon, you know, that place in the sky where it shines brighter than all my troubles? I hope to meet you there one day..

**Playing games with
my heart:
effeuiller la marguerite.
Un peu or beaucoup,
passionnément or à la folie,
or pas du tout?**

(He loves me, he loves me not. A little or a lot.
Passionately, or to madness, or not at all..)

Sometimes I imagine you here with me, your head upon my heart, listening to the rhythm of mine beating for you..

I could breathe you in every day and never once tire of thee..

He had power in his bones, for he awoke sleeping butterflies and made my heart smile with just his existence alone.

Midnight skies and evergreens, cleansing raindrops and other things, birdsong that carries away my rue, morning blades of grass covered in dew, but none come close to the way I'm moved by just the simple existence of you.

You are my muse..

If you silence your mind long enough, you can hear her calling for you.

Shh, quiet now..

Even angels with broken wings can still fly. It only takes two, you and I.

I may not be
the most
beautiful apple
in the orchard,
but I'm still
ripe and ready
to fall.

Anything forced will never remain.
Allow all things to flow freely as they should.

For those of you who struggle to silence your mind, I offer you a pen, some paper, and a seat at my table.

There's so much more to silence than just pain.

Listen..

I'm glad we ended well. I'm glad because there's a certain peace that comes with that. To know you're okay, we're okay, even if it's not together, it's all going to be okay.

You are worthy. You are deserving of tenderness and love. Fuck people who tell you otherwise; they're obviously misinformed. No one knows you better than you do your own self, so if someone is filling your head full of that filth, just remember it has nothing to do with you but everything to do with who they are as a person. Don't let people's opinions sway you. Stand strong. You are worthy. Always. Always. Always. Never forget that.

Before sending that 'I miss you' message, remember, you wouldn't be missing them at all if they felt the same.

But can they
make your heart
smile, though?

Be careful, oh my soul, of those who take, but very seldom give.

His mouth did murder me at every single turn as I sat silently bearing the burden of heartbreak.

*Abuse

You feel her!? You don't feel shit! You couldn't even feel your own heart quiver if your life depended on it.

My love is unconditional.
My devotion, however, is not.

Her whispers are starting to get loud, and her screams are no longer quiet. She's no longer willing to sit locked away inside of this cage you put her in, hushed alone in the silence. Fear, for the Phoenix in her, is rising.

Love is not always silent. Sometimes, it claws at your mind, and no matter how much you pack it in ice to soothe the ache, somehow, it still manages to leave you frozen.

If being a bitch means getting tired of the bullshit and standing up for yourself, then so be it. I'll wear that title proudly along with this fire in my eyes that so beautifully matches my sundress.

I love with my heart
torn wide open. You
just love being loved.
We're not the same.

She was never asking for a yes man, just one that cared.

Your person is your partner, one who walks beside you, not your child to be ordered around. You cannot make demands in a relationship and then get angry at them for not obeying. You make requests, allowing them the freedom to choose. Then, whatever they choose, you respect that decision and them as a person, which will enable them to be comfortable with being themselves. They are allowed to disagree respectfully. In those instances, compromises should be made. This is the part where the two attempt to find a middle ground or agree to disagree but always doing so in love.

(how it should be)

It wasn't what you did
but what you didn't do
that hurt the most.

Kindness is no candor if it's laced with poison.

If they love you, they will ALWAYS find a way; if not, they'll be sure to offer an excuse.

"Hurt, people, hurt people," is not always true, for I can testify to many who have stumbled upon ruins that have plagued their souls. Still, they took those catastrophes, allowing their heart to become more tender, that another would never have to suffer the same. Not everyone will break you: there are some who will cradle you most tenderly. So, please, never lose hope, sweet one.

Very much a part of the all, was he, that when his soul was weeping, even the ground shook and the sky ripped open to flood us with her salty tears.

(how oceans were created)

3 am
I watched the
streetlight burn
out this
morning, and I
could feel the
ache in my
heart of
missing you..

It's not enough for me to fuck it up. No, I've got to burn it all the way down to the ground; I'm like fire; you can't embrace me.

This is me in all my non-glory; love me, or just stay the fuck away.

Let's go back to the way things were before.. Before I opened my fucking mouth wide and screwed up all you held inside. Let's go back, shall we? Erase it all, save for the friendship we had before the fall? Take me back? I don't want to sit in the absence of you anymore.

If you ask me how I'm doing, I'm not going to say 'fine' if I'm not just to keep you comfortable. No, I will tell you that my bones are aching, that I am broken and feel utterly alone. I will not lie to keep you around or because you can't handle feelings. No, you will either care, or it will all just fall to the ground.

I am like fire, burning down all that I touch, and can never seem to hold in my hands that which I long for so much. It all becomes but ashes beneath the soles of my tired feet, and there's nothing much left save this longing and..
I miss you.

I always seem to win at losing, not this game of life, but you.

Just give me a lighthouse out
on the sea,
with nothing but waves
silently washing over me.

A place away from the noise
of it all,
where I can feel the
moonlight on my skin,
and lie in grassy fields,
making friends with
the wind..

Allowing it to carry me,
and all my troubles,
far, far, away from here.

I got you; I heard your words, and I understood them, every one, for I, too, have a tendency of breaking it all to the ground. Never my intentions, but listening as those words fell so softly on the soul of my heart, maybe friendships really are better. Things don't seem to fall so much apart as they would with a lover. See, friends accept you as you are and all things just flow. Lovers, well, they have expectations, and that just kind of ruins everything, you know?

Sometimes, the lessons learned in life are tough ones, and sometimes, I could give myself a swift kick in the backside for not getting things right, especially when I knew better the first time.

There is nothing heavier in life to carry around than the weight of a shattered heart.

Can we just hit the button on time, rewind, and go back to the days of innocents, where days ran longer, and there was an adventure in everything?

Just give me back over to the sea. I don't much like those who beat down bare feet on barren, dry land anymore.

I have always loved with my heart torn wide open, never fearing the fall, and although that has brought on much pain, I shall continue that path, for I know no other way at all.

I see you. I know your pain. I understand the horrors suffered at the hands of broken people. Innocence lost. Love crushed underfoot. Pain beyond the ability to comprehend, and it turned you into passion, into light, into a beacon for humanity, one that pulls them out of the pits of despair. You are needed. Your light is most necessary for those still in hell, those who still face darkness and despair alone. You make a difference. You matter. Keep going.

You create your destiny by what you think, for your thoughts are seeds, and if you give too much energy to them, they reach your heart, and from the abundance of the heart, the mouth speaks.
Those words are living and active; they have the power to create and also to destroy.

Even further than that, be careful who you surround yourself with because you become like the company you keep, and in that becoming, you are forming habits that are hard to break.

With all this, your character is molded, and you have your personality. Small things have a significant impact, for they create your destiny. So please, be careful in all things. Guard your thoughts, your heart, your tongue, and your circle most carefully because these are the things that make up your life.

The power of becoming lies within you.

All things come to those who find the courage to believe.

If ever there was a
mountain to be
moved, she would be
the one to do it.

For A.A.G.🌹

We accomplish more together than we ever could apart.

(Villages people, villages..)

Sometimes, I make friends; others, I make enemies, but always, I make it a point to offer goodness to them both.

I'm far too happy being genuinely happy to stop and seek any validation at all.

believe in yourself, in
your own natural
abilities that make you
unique and powerful to
this world. it is
necessary for the
coloring of life..

I won't settle for a mundane life. I lust for depth, the deeper things hidden within the cracks of people's souls for it is there that I find the beauty in living, the strength to continue on one more day, and the love that carries my wearied, wounded soul..

most loves will wilt
like every flower they
give, but one day,
someday, there will
come one that does
not pluck the petals
from their existence,
but just tends the
garden instead..

I'm glad I live in a world where there is YOU.

Even if I only ever had but one tender moment with you, it would be enough for me, enough to hold me for longer than eternity.

You will always have
a home in my heart,
no matter how far
you may roam.

Wherever your mind goes when it wanders off, that place of peace that you find when your soul is quieted within you, that's what matters. Focus on that.

Unpopular opinion

It isn't called soulmate; it's called euphoria. Wait until the veil has been stripped away and the faults are revealed; see if they stay. That's when you know it's real.

Even sky is weeping this night. The stars have all hidden their face, and the moon refuses to glow.

Different

If I had a choice in the matter, it would have all been..

I can't do much for
you from the grave,
so please, while I live,
let me love you.

Sorrow

As heavy as it may be, it is still critical to the understanding of happiness.

I was in love with a moment, a tender and most precious moment that only existed in my mind.

What magical alchemy of senses it would be if two givers were to meet and fall in love.

Gentle, soft touches to the heart, and you'll have hers forever.

You deserve the same effort you give.

Love seeks to take care of its own in all ways, always.

You are your own..

And sometimes, strong wears out, and you have to allow yourself to break. Just don't forget to get back up when you're finished.

Rest

A short interlude to find
some much-needed peace
for hearts that carry
sorrows much heavier
than themselves.

Have a day;
whatever kind
of day you
need to have
to be okay.

Had it not been
for the tragedies,
I might never
have given birth
to kindness.

I am not love and light. I carry around a bag full of heavy, broken bones, but I learned to become like love and light so that others do not have to suffer the same.

Little did they know that when they split me open, I would bleed love.

I got you, I do. But what if they don't want to be got? Then you exercise patience, acceptance, and respect their decisions. Respect their way of doing things, and let them do what they need to do for them because if you really do care about someone, the only thing you'll ever want is for them to be okay. Even more than that, you'll wish for them to smile, to feel love, and let happiness kiss their cheek no matter what form it may come to them in, even if that isn't with you.

Pay more attention to their actions, not their words. As much as you want to believe the things they say, how they treat you will always be how they feel about you..

I had too much hope
in my bones to
believe the truth of
just how fruitless
your words actually
were, for I believed
far too much in you.

Grief

It is a slow, maddening torture to care so deeply for someone and have to watch helplessly as they slowly pull away.

My own personal hell..

Happily never after..

Story of my life

Why is it that people have to break things off on bad terms? Why can't things be handled civilly? Why can't two people say bye and wish the other one well? Why can't things be worked out in an adult manner? Fuck all that extra shit. Life is too short, and time is far too precious to be wasting energy on people who lack the ability to communicate in a respectful manner. That is all.

You know you've leveled up and reached a dangerously awesome place of freedom when you no longer get sad when people walk out on you. Let em' walk and fight it not, for the ones who are meant to be there will always remain. No negotiation necessary.

I have no one to blame but myself, for what I allowed continuously repeated itself until I decided to stop fighting my ego and grow.

Accountability

There's this wall built around my heart that others have placed there, lined with different colored bricks reading things like abandonment, dismissive, invalidation, silent treatment, lack of concern, lack of understanding, ghosting, crazy-making, and every other abusive tactic known to man. I am growing quite exhausted from trying to break them down one by one. Let them build the wall, higher and higher, and I'll just sit inside there with my solitude and the peace that comes without the bullshit.

Sometimes you just have to hold on to the music because that's all that's left holding you.

So this is what hell looks like - riding on the backs of fools?

An apology that contains an excuse is no apology at all, for there's a certain growth that can be found in holding one's self accountable.

Let it go—
a nice way of shutting one down. Filed under dismissive or gaslighting.

Let it go—
a release, setting one free. Filed under forgiveness or deliverance, but only after the topic at hand has been taken care of. Huge difference.

Sometimes, I'm brave. Other times, I feel like a terrified squirrel attempting to try and figure out how the hell to cross the busy street without getting run over. Either way, I'm still here, pushing forward and doing it afraid because both have lessons to teach, and I am here to learn and grow, no matter how terrifying that may be.

Sometimes, I think the hardest person for us to love is ourselves.

Sometimes, life teaches us kindness in the most unkind of ways, love in the most unloving ways, and happiness in a form that is not so sweet.

Love is not always soft,
sometimes it's hard and
heavy, and you have to ask
yourself if you're willing
to still choose that person
over and over again,
despite the tough times..
because that's what love is
really all about, a constant
choosing every single day.

To love them, you much go past the light, beyond the surface of their skin, and dive deep into the darkest pits of their soul; making a home there, a place where they feel safe with you and comfortable in their own skin. You must show them that loving them means to teach them to love themselves, all of who they are, just as you do.

Truths are primarily based on the opinions of the masses of people that are just trying not to be wrong.

Imagine a world where people actually held themselves accountable.

This is my heart, and I know you don't understand her, but if you'll but listen with yours, she'll tell you all you need to know.

She doesn't open
her heart up to
just anyone,
so if she just so
happens to,
you should
probably listen.

That's the thing with
being real,
some will love you,
and others will love to
hate you.
Neither changes
that truth.
It all lies in how well they
can accept it.

If you are here, just being the you
that nobody wants you to be,
and loving yourself still because no
one else ever would.
If you spend your
days lifting your own self up,
drying your own tears,
pulling your own self up by the
bootstraps,
and carrying on-
then you, my friend,
you are brave, beautiful, and so
damn strong for that.
Brave, beautiful you.
You'll see.
Keep moving forward in that.
I'm so very proud of you.

For me, you will always be enough.

If heaven does exist, please, let it be you.

What you do for my heart
can only be understood by
explaining the story of the
first night when stars
were born,
tenderly bursting forth
their glow in a darkened,
midnight sky, and it was
very good, gentle, and all
things lovely.

You are the most beautiful thing I've never known.

And suddenly,
all of the words became about
HIM.

Hang on to her hand in the same way she holds on to your heart, for she does not disappoint.

If you think I don't feel you, I do. God, I fucking do! Every piece of energy that radiates from your soul, it captivates me. I'm am lost in the all that makes up that you, and I don't want to be found by anyone, anyone that is save for you.

You touch places in
my heart that I didn't
even know existed.

The more I learn about you, the deeper I fall.

He is the sweetest love story that my heart has ever known. Like a breath of fresh air from a cool morning breeze, he sends me so beautifully to my knees.

And each day,
you take me to
that beautiful
place that others
can only dream of.

A million and
one people
pulling me this
way and that,
but my eyes are
only ever
looking for him.

Sweet angel of love, fear not, for even in the toughest of times, I will still be there loving you.

Sometimes, you just have to take that risk. Sure, you might get your heart broken, but it is far better than giving up the try. Who knows, they could just be the one who makes your soul fly? Do not allow yourself to miss out on something good just because it scares you. Some of the most beautiful things in life are found outside of our comfort zones.

They don't like it when I fall in love because when I do, I tumble head first with all of my soul and usually, I end up getting hurt. That's okay with me because the adventures, they were great. It will make for wonderful stories to tell my grandchildren. A life well lived, and one done so without fear. A heart that was brave enough to take on every form of love and it was beautiful. Maybe it will inspire them to never give up hope; to take up their courage and live. What else is this life for if not to experience things in all of their untamed beauty? I hope that they live, and I mean really fucking live. Yeah, I'm going to be one of those grandmas that cuss, and not only that but one who slides sideways into her grave knowing that I gave it my all right up until the day that I breathed my very last.

Even if I never get to touch your face, to feel the warmth of your breath on my skin, it was worth it, this feeling. It is one like I have never known before. So bright, so brilliant, so out of this world-

You have been one to set my soul free to soar like Icarus, higher than the angels do fly, and it has been nothing less than an absolute pleasure to fall for its melting.

Sitting out here on the front porch of a Sunday's morning rise, I watch the leaves as they all clap their hands in unison to their Maker as if to say thank you for the cool, gentle breeze. Then, suddenly, one falls, and it does so with such elegance and grace, dancing along as it goes. Allowing itself to freefall, it surrenders its life and simply goes with the flow as it takes its final plunge towards death. Now there's this other one that clings to a half dew-covered spider web. It twists and turns, holding on for dear life to the last bit of breath it has before becoming one with the earth again. And I'm not sure exactly what it's trying to say, but I believe, maybe, I was supposed to watch that? Perhaps, I'm to let loose of that thin thread I grasp so tightly to and flow with the natural occurrences of life. Things seem to be more beautiful that way, at least with nature anyways.

Ladies, take care of your man. Sometimes, something as simple as an uplifting and encouraging message is all they need to give them that little extra push they need to make it through. Men go through so much that most won't even say. So please, make sure you let him know how very proud of him you are and how very much you appreciate all that he does. Little things such as these go a long way and have such a significant impact on their spirit. Take care of your man, and he will take care of all that is you. Simple.

Breathe life into wounded souls. Pick them up from off their knees. Show them that not everyone is the same; that there are ones who do care, who's hearts are whiter than snow. Why? Because you've been there, a million and one times, and there was no one to do it for you. Love, with every beat of your broken heart and then some so that others may not have to suffer the same.

We have to
TAKE CARE OF
ONE ANOTHER
if we're going to
survive this
thing we call life.

If 'the love of money is the root of all evil,' then selfishness must be its brother.

If it is in your power, love hard, love big, and take care of the ones who cross your path. You may be the only one who ever does. Life is full of selfish souls; make it a point to be the opposite of that.

I've been walked out on so many times in my life that I don't even get sad anymore; disappointed yes, but sad, no. Let em' walk. I know in my heart of hearts that the right one will always stay.

When we try to remember, we forget. When we try to forget, we remember.

Take a breath of life.
In every breath lies death.
Take a breath of death.

One day, she just stopped...

I had too much love
in my bones to
believe the truth of
just how fruitless
your words
actually were, and
the release was
even slower still..

Spend time on me or don't. I'll learn to live with or without you either way.

Actions will always be louder than words. Figure it out. It has nothing to do with proving yourself. Things like this come naturally, and if your lady is worth it to you and you see value in her, you will provide the actions that line up with your words. That is all.

Communication is so damn important in a relationship. You should have the ability to talk to your partner about anything, but if you find yourself feeling worse after every attempt, then just stop because they probably don't give a fuck. If you are speaking up for your needs and they aren't being dealt with, then run. Run away as fast as you can and never look back, not for a second.

You're going to look at her, and that from a distance.. and suddenly, you're going to see how fucking bright she lights up the entire midnight sky. You're going to wish you had breathed her in, that the scales that blinded you had fallen off of your eyes a little bit sooner; that you had held her tighter than all the troubles that had the power to grow the two of you stronger. You're going to see her in all of her glory; you're going to see her strength of heart and the way she carries tenderness to the skies, and you're going to miss her. You're just going to have to fucking miss her.

Oh, the many times I tried to teach this old heart of mine how to stop caring, but she is a fighter and would not have it that way. No, she would insist that I feel every damn thing, and that to the bone.

You just can't communicate with people who only want to see things from their level of perception. Ones who get angry at you for having a difference of opinion. In conversation, you must be willing to slip another's soul on and try to understand their world, how they see things. That's how we get a wide variety of knowledge. That's how we gain understanding. That is so simple and yet, so very seldomly done.

I speak in terms of energy. If you want to understand me, feel me.

I can handle the truth just fine no matter how hard it may be; you just couldn't handle mine.

If you're doing something for someone, thinking you may get something in return, you're not really doing it for them, but yourself and for your own selfish gain. Love does not seek its own, but happily looks after another. It will desire to give freely from the heart because it cares about you and genuinely wants to see you happy. Do it from the heart, or don't even do it at all.

I was introduced to evil at a very young age, and I had to choose: did I want to become like ugly or mature and be kind? I chose tenderness. I spent my days smothering others with it, for I knew the pain of the falling and was not willing to be one who added that kind of weight to another human soul, no matter what the circumstances may have been. And that has been the biggest blessing but also the most painful heartache of my entire life.

Sometimes, life hands us gifts like kindness, love, and strength, but not always in the way we think.

You feel as if you're drowning, but if you will but simply grab her hand, she'll teach you how to breathe through deep waters.

I shall love them, every one, no matter how far I may fall. I shall clinch them up tight in my hands, for I know no other way at all.

I need laughter,
and kindness,
and tender
places to fall. I
am tired.

Sometimes, strong wears out, and you just gotta do it worn.

Because sometimes, you just want to lay your head in their lap and rest a while, that's all.

Those who love deeply,
hurt deeply too.

Sometimes, strong wears out, and you just have to do it worn.

The ones that are always carrying others also need to be lifted at times.

I love too hard. I care too deeply. I have an endless supply of passion that resides inside of my bones, and sometimes I feel like it's just too damn much to ask anyone to take on. As so, I waste away alone.

So this is what it's like, Jesus, to have an endless love and to be surrounded by those who cannot receive it in full? There's so much love that it hurts. I can only give it in bits, a piece here, a smidgen there, but what shall I do with the rest of it when there's no one left to give it to? At the end of the day, I'm alone, and I have all this love stuck inside of me that's aching to be free, and it just turns to pain. So what is it that I'm supposed to do with what remains?

The key to my
heart is tucked
into God's pocket.
If you want me,
you have to go
through Him.

Be careful with her, sweet one. She may just be the one who laughs, loves, and saves you on your tough days when you're struggling to survive.

Surely we must have been together in a previous lifetime. Why else, when I look at you, do you feel like home to me?

He is not like the others, for he is an ancient, rare soul belonging to the wisdom of the trees, the whispers of the wind, to the glow of the moon, the stones of the Earth, to the scent of jasmine, the sound of crickets chirping, to the song of the bird, and to the colors of the sky.

I asked the universe for a hug, and it sent me you.

And some things in this world are too damn lovely even to attempt to find words for; you are one of them.

You make me
feel the way
music does.

I love you. It's all I know.
The rest is history.

Do not let that man go..
You only get one great man
in life. There may be other
good guys too, but there's
only one great man that
you'll never forget for the
rest of your life, I promise
you. Don't let him go. Do
whatever it takes to keep
him because you will regret
letting him walk away.

You know what I appreciate: People who pay attention. Those genuine souls that take notice of the little things that matter to you.

What use is all this love, the depth within these bones if there is not one with which to share it? Tis but a curse. A curse, I say! To love without limits and live in a world full of guarded, wounded, and fearful souls. At the end of the day, I stand alone. A heart full of love and only but the trees to hold me. People come, they take what they need, and then they go. Do they not know there's so much more to give? Take me whole and soak in the depth of me because this well will never run dry. Alone I die. Tis but a curse, a curse I say, to be so full of love and to live in a world where I have not one to give it to completely. Despair has finally got its hold on me, and this time, I don't think it's letting go. I weep. I weep. I weep.
Alone.

Let them go, honey. You will never have to fight for a position in someone's life if they want you there.

Let people have their opinions and walk away with your peace. There's no need to try and convince anyone of your heart.

Observe those tears.
Take notice of the way your bones are splintered and cracked and yet you still bleed love.
Do you see the way you wake up each day to face another sun regardless?
That's called strength of heart.
Keep going, beautiful soul.

Practice the art not of letting go, but of acceptance and allowing all things to flow.

Even if I never get to touch your face or feel the warmth of your breath on my skin, it was worth it, this feeling. It is one like I have never known before. So bright, so brilliant, so out of this world-
You have been one to set my soul free to soar like Icarus, higher than the angels do fly, and it has been nothing less than an absolute pleasure to fall for its melting.

Heaven does exist, for I found its song residing right there inside of his precious, soft, beating heart.

There is no greater
joy in life to be had
than to taste what
it feels like when
the soul of another
does smile.

Have you ever been hustling along in a rush to do your business, and a sudden, cool breeze hits your face Instantaneously, you pause, close your eyes, and soak in it for a moment? That is him, a soft, gentle breeze.

I don't know why our paths crossed. All I know is that I like the way my soul feels when I'm around you, and that feeling, you, I hope it never goes away. Stay.

How lovely is the hour in which the sun doth kiss the sky goodnight, but I can't help but wonder how much more beauty could be added to it if I could but share the same with you?

I twisted my breath
into a lasso and flung
it up past the moon
catching the last star
where I entered
heaven and rested
softly in his arms.

You deserve to be loved.Not liked. Not lusted after. Not used. Not settled for, but loved. Really and truly loved. Never forget it!

Sometimes it rains while the sun is shining, and sometimes it's like that inside people's hearts too.

I am flowers strewn about a haunted house.

If the love of money is the root of all evil, then expectation is its brother.

Sometimes, some of the prettiest smiles hold the deepest scars, and the kindest people have the most battered hearts.

Sometimes, life is not so simple. It is tough, and hard, and cruel, and unkind. There are days it just sucks the life right out of you. Just know that every step you take is leading you somewhere. You are making progress that is taking you in the right direction, even if it doesn't feel that way. Keep going, beautiful soul. I believe in you.

Imagine hurting the soul that God sent to heal you.

Don't be just lucky to have them, be deserving.

It's okay, I'm used to it.

Saddest three words in
the history of humanity:
I miss you..

Can we go back to the days of innocence? Days when we hadn't a care in the world aside from playing in the dirt, or waiting for our favorite song to come on and just sit with it forever? I want to go back. Take me back. Let's go back, shall we?

Do not settle because there will be one to come along one day that will kiss you like the fire in the sky does the horizon at night. Wait for them.

I once wanted to be the
woman that changed the
whole world, but at the
end of the day, my soul is
tired, and all I want is just
to come home to you.

I need not power, nor riches, no, I need not even be right—
Just your love, that is all, that's enough.

You make for good
memories,
something
beautiful to tuck
up under my ribs.

She could spend her time however she wanted, but all she ever wanted was to spend it with you.

I love you more than
I'll ever find the
courage to say. All I
know is, I hope that
you can stay.

What magical alchemy of senses it would be if two givers were to meet and fall in love.

Dare to dream..

No one loves harder than those who have suffered mercilessly at the hands of selfish souls.

I'll always hold your heart just a little bit tighter than I did the day before. Always.

You're holding it in your hands-

My Heart

Seven billion people on this planet, and I have the privilege of meeting you.

Dare to be
DIFFERENT

Perception is huge on
this planet.
Having the ability to step out of
your own soul and into
someone else's and to see life
through
the eyes of their heart are most
necessary if we're going to
survive on this planet.

1+4=5, but so is 2+3.

Relationships are not complex. All you have to do is care and continue looking after their heart long after the euphoria has worn away for always. If your love is genuine, for you, this will be simple.

Let your love be so pure, so real, so big, and so loud that it shifts the whole damn frequency of the planet.

Life is not complicated. You
have your opinion, and I
have
mine, and we're both right,
so let's find
common ground or agree
to disagree
while still remaining
friends, shall we? See?
It's simple.

It's okay that you
do not know, but at
some point, it
becomes your duty
to figure it out.

She is the type of woman who would have believed in you for longer than eternity, and one day, you're going to look back and see that, but by then, it will be too late.

If any one of you has ever had to walk away from someone you love because they weren't so kind to you, I am so sorry. Please know that I am proud of you for choosing you. That takes strength and courage of heart. Each day you will get better and better. There will be times when it all falls heavy on your shoulders, but keep going. You are brave, beautiful, and you are loved. Remember, all the magic you saw in them, it was really your magic you were seeing all along. Keep going, and going, and going. Eventually, that mountain will be in the distance, and you will be proud of how far you've come. One moment at a time, brave soul.

Rise, Phoenix. Rise!

The heart is the only thing that will keep on working long after it's been shattered to pieces, and that is the tragedy of living.

I need laughter,
and kindness, and
tender places to
fall. I am tired.

Music has the power to change your relationship with pain.

And when reality hurt too much, I could always find myself tangled up in beautiful thoughts of you.

There are some days that you'll
want to succumb
to the fear, the anxiety, the doubt,
the sorrow that bleeds you dry,
but I pray that you don't. I
hope you keep fighting with every
ounce of fire in your soul. Even
when it's hard, even when it's
tough, keep going. You just keep
going and
pushing. This too will eventually
pass and the
light will shine again. Hold tight
to the fight!

I have always loved
too much, too hard,
and way too deep,
and that has always
been my tragedy.

If they're interested in you, you'll know. There won't be a single doubt in your mind.

And she lived happily ever after with her own self and her books that accompanied her on wild and beautiful adventures.

I saw the face of God today when that stranger smiled at me on the street.
And I felt the gentle touch of His hands when my sister dried my tired eyes and, with care, wrapped her loving arms around me. I heard Him in birdsong; I felt Him in the wind, and He was right there when a kind word was offered from a friend. He's always there; He's everywhere. And I am thankful for eyes with which to see. Thank you, God, for loving me.

I just really need to stop a moment and appreciate all the souls who have ever tasted of hell. The one's who have know tragedy and not allowed that darkness to turn them bitter. Thank you for taking all that heartbreak, all the weight of sorrow, and turning it into something good. Thank you for the love and kindness you so selflessly instill into others. You are a brave soul for that, a beautiful person indeed. Brave, beautiful you. That is all.

I think my soul sits right there in the middle of my chest for when I am sad, I can feel her there aching as she works her way up to my throat and eventually out of my eyes again.

There's a forest in my mind, and often times I go there when things are becoming dark, and there I will sit beneath the willows as birds perch on my soul, carrying me far, far away from it all to a magical place where all their songs go when sung, and I am comforted.

Come, my love,
dress me in your
softest song, for my
heart is wounded
and bare. Come.

A whisper of a lost poem, my breath falling softly into your heart, and then to the floor. Oh flame, burn me brighter than the moon for my pulse has a thousand wings all wrapped in silk for you.

Still waiting for the wind that won't come, your breath far from my reach. Sweet lover of my soul, how far as the stars you are from me, but in my heart, I still hold you close and see you glisten as the moon.

Do not try and explain
your soul to anyone.
You only need to know
her yourself. To
everyone else, you are
but a reflection.

You're beautiful, and you have a good heart. Some people are just too damn blinded by their own extreme to even notice.

Pay no attention to those people who say, 'don't be sad.' Fuck that, be sad. Sit with it, feel it, cry it out and wash it from your soul, whatever it is that you need to do until you feel okay again. Then, let it go and smile that beautiful smile. I got you, I'm here, I care, and I'm with you all the way.

I wish we could run out of emotions like we run out of gas.

The path of love may not always be easy, but I can assure you, it's always the right way to go.

My idea of
love went
extinct with
the dinosaurs
eons ago.

It's not enough to just love them; you have to be willing to move oceans and flip this world upside down should love call for it.

You claim to want things, so many things, but do you actually move your feet in that direction, doing things and reaching for them with both hands?

Keep on moving forward to that which you so long for, even if it hasn't happened for you just yet. You will get there soon enough.

Persistent

Reality is but a hallucination, a simple mirror of your own beliefs.

Never did I carry
the weight of
anything heavier
than that of my
own soul.

If you wish to learn anything in this life, anything at all, ask for karma to greet you, not your enemy. Seek revenge only upon your own self.

People are constantly
battling the outside
world, but it's the insides
that are hurting so much.
If they'd but focus their
attention on that, the
world would be an
entirely different place.

Everything I learned about forever was taught to me by those who were always saying goodbye.

Take me back to the days of old because I don't much like this world's idea of love anymore.

The saddest thing about having a kind heart and loving deeply beyond all measure: you'll walk your path alone. It is only but the ancients and old souls that have the ability to meet you on that level, and they went extinct with the dinosaurs.

I will be different because everyone else is too much the same.

And she would change a thousand times before the setting of the sun.

I've been through too much to continue to surround myself with those who do not care at all. I need tenderness, soft places to fall, and if one cannot offer that, then just stay away from me. That is all.

No one educates us on self-love. We are taught to deny ourselves, but how can you give to another if you don't first fill yourself? Let not your cup be empty, but fill it to the brim so that it may spill over onto another, my friend. A well-nourished heart nourishes, and in the garden of our souls, is where it all begins.

I hope that when I slide sideways into my grave, that my journey here on Earth made things a little lighter for someone. I hope that my existence made someone else find their own strength to push through just one more day. I hope that my presence lifted the corners of someone's sagging smile a little higher, even if it was just a moment. And I hope that love was something I continuously handed over to another human soul, regardless of the circumstances. For what else is this life for, save to pass beauty on to another before we breathe our last?

Moments come, and they do go; they slip right through our fingertips, but we can always hold on to the memories. We can hang them forever in the walls of our hearts and keep a candle burning for those with which we must part until we can meet up with them once more. Forever, I'll be loving you.

There are clouds
in my mind again,
and I don't wish to
come down.

I twisted my breath
into a lasso and flung
it up past the moon,
catching the last star
and rode it to heaven
where I rested softly
in your arms.

Waves of love and sweet joy fill my heart and begin to leak from my eyes at the very though of you.

Whisper soft kisses upon my tongue. Set the stars in my eyes, my love. Remember me.

When I love,
I love hard.
When I break,
I do that
even harder.

Be present, be aware, for life is lived one single moment at a time.

Just remember,
you're beautiful and
worthy of love and
kindness. Anyone
who makes you feel
otherwise is not
worth your time or
your tears. Keep
moving forward.

Being there for your lady does not always mean fixing her problems. Sometimes, it's as simple as giving her a hand to hold or a shoulder to rest on until things become light again. Little things such as these let her know she's not alone and that you care. She is strong and brave enough to resolve her issues on her own. Just being there is all that is really required.

Speaking up for your needs is not picking a man apart. If they say that, it's their own internal, undealt with trauma, or they do not care. You are a part of the relationship, too, and your needs are valid, especially to those who care. Keep loving yourself and using your voice. You're important also.

Take me back to the days of old, where men took care of their families? A time when women respected their men. Take me to that place where the falling was easy, marriages were cherished, and people had a forever in mind. Take me back, please, to that beautiful place of old and hold me there.

To love someone is to love them whole, crooked halo and all.

I do believe in
karma but only
wish it upon my
own self, for I
still have so very
much to learn,
no matter how
far I've come.

Sometimes, I feel like fire, wanting to embrace all that I see but burning down all that I touch, everything I lay my heart to, and when I look around, there's nothing left but me and all these ashes beneath the soles of my tired feet.

See, that's the thing with angels who were fashioned in Hell; they burn people, but never on purpose.

I am still
learning that
not everything
requires a
response.

Love will always
reach for your
heart first. It will
be willing to take
care of all that is
you, including the
tough things that
others so carelessly
left behind.

When all else fails, love yourself, for there's not a soul on this planet that can do that better than you.

Sorrow of heart is sitting next to your person and feeling utterly alone. Contentment is not giving a fuck and enjoying your own company regardless.

Would you miss them if they were gone? Then they're a blessing. Remember that and treat them well.

You always hated
your black wings
and crooked halo,
but little did you
know, they were my
favorite color, and
that halo, damn, you
wore it so well.

I longed to embrace his darkness, for the moonlight twinkled on his skin, and the soft glow that surrounded him left me breathless.

You would think the sun rose and fell in his eyes, the way she looked at him.

Hemingway said,
"All you
have to do is write
one true
sentence."

Truth:
I love you.

When your cheeks hurt from smiling so much, that's when you know you've got it good. These moments are really hard to come by, but l assure you, they will come. And when they do, make damn sure to nurture the soul that brought on all of that joy, and take care of their heart for as long as life will allow.

It's all about who
you think
about when you
close your eyes;
the one that
makes the rest of
the world kind of
fade away.

It's in the little things, always in the little things. Like the way they listen and show genuine interest in what you have to say. It's in the way that they pull you in close when your world is caving in. it's the 'i got yous,' the smiles, the laughs, and the small moments that make you feel seen that show you they care the most. These are the precious moments that turn into memories that we hang on the walls of our hearts. It may not seem like much to some, but to me, it's everything.

We shared our hearts in spring, and all things did bloom, then winter came and stripped away the veil, and all of what made up us of us was consumed. And that's okay, because winter will teach you who will go and who will stay, and the wise know it is only but a season, for love will not betray. Hearts will bloom once more and be warmed by a summer's soft breeze, and even if they fall again, they understand it's a constant choosing every single day. For with love, you must be ever ready to change with each season and grow with the flow; it is only but a moment in time, you know?

Life is short. Things change at the drop of a hat. Do not let one day slip by without offering those that you care for flowers, flowers of kindness, of peace, and that of love. We all deserve that, to know that we're important, that we're valued, and that somewhere in this big wide world, there was someone who cared. Regret lasts a lifetime, so please, give those flowers of kindness out today.

Try not to worry so much; it all comes out as it should in the end anyways. Be as water and let it flow.

Happiness cannot be found in fancy cars and diamond rings. No, it exists somewhere between the light and the darkness. It is in the little moments where kindness rests and where there are soft places to fall. Beauty isn't found in what one has, but in the gentleness that they can give, planting it into the hearts of
many, even when they're not so kind, because for me, this is where heaven exists, where forever lives.

kiss me softly
like autumn
🍂 does the
trees when
everything
is dying. 🍂

She was born soft in a hard and cruel world. She wore strength well and burned with a beautiful spirit that not many could contend with, for when they offered up hatred, she simply transformed it into love, and not many knew what to do with that.

Heaven begins with kindness, a tiny seed that is planted in a heart that they, too, can pass along to another. It is a tenderness that just keeps going on for forever.

There is a window that leads to my soul that most cannot see. They're lost, and so, all that remains is this misunderstanding or judgment of me that looks much like themselves.

I've been tilling the soil of my heart for a while now and planting flowers where the heartache use to be, but every time they bloom, someone comes along plucking their petals one by one, singing some song, curiously wondering about whether someone loves them, or loves them not. And I sure hope that they do for my sake because I'm all out of seeds.

They told me to stay inside the lines, so I made sure I went four extra miles to color outside of them.

My goal has been, and always will be, to bring joy to those I care for. No games, no bullshit, just smiles. Life is hard enough as it is. If you find someone who seeks only to bring happiness into yowr world, one who wishes for nothing but joy for you, even when it's hard, if they're still there trying to you underytand you through anger and the hard things, you'd better hang tight because people don't exist like that much anymore. If you find them, love them hard for as long as life will allow.

What a blessing and a privilege it has been to step outside of myself and love other souls. Although it comes with great pain, I wouldn't have traded it for anything. I am blessed to know God in many forms, and He is so very good.

I am tough, but I am tired.

My darling, all I want is for you to be happy, to smile that beautiful smile every day, and to know that somewhere in this big wide world, there was someone who loved you with every beat of their soul.

Love is
wanting what's
best for them,
even if that
doesn't include
you.

Here is what I know:
Love is the answer to
all things, and love..
love is pain. If you are
looking for love, be
willing to bleed.

When life is beating down on you, turn up the music, it will always get you through.

Music is the
gentle whispers
and breath of
the soul.

She had been through tragedy of every kind, and that is what fashioned her into a deep, empathetic soul. She was not willing to see a one of them fall without doing her absolute best to raise them from up off their knees. No one could care for you like her, no one. That woman would flip this world upside down and drink the ocean dry to keep you from drowning if that's what life and love called for. This is what she chooses to do with all the heartache handed to her on knives she painfully tore from her back, and she was blessed for it. Blessed with seeing smiles and joy light up in the faces of many. This is what she breaths for; this is why she loves. She may not have been able to unbreak her own heart, but it was in the gentle smiles of others that it was slowly being healed. And she loved them for it.

All I ever asked God for was a family, not riches or fancy things, just a full complete family that I could call my own. One's that I could care for and give every ounce of myself to in all things, but He would not have it that way, no. God saw that my heart was much too big, and there was just too much love in there for one household alone. So instead, He gave me the world, and I have loved them so. Even when they beat me, even when they spat in my face, I loved them still with every ounce of me, and I am thankful. Maybe in the next life, He can grant me what I so longed for? Maybe?

Come, my love, to
the garden of my
soul where you
can pick flowers
of love that will
never wilt. Come.

There will never be a single day that goes by in which I don't gaze upon you and realize how blessed that I truly am.

Heaven is:
Feeling the
warmth of his
smile against
my lips.

How lucky I am that the Lord should bless me with the morning and waking up just to fall in love with you all over again.

Loving you is
something I
will never
take lightly.

My heart blooms twice
when you kiss me first.

Her love language cannot be found in I or in reading a how-to book, although that may help. No, it is found nestled inside of her soft, beating heart. Listen to it with yours, and your questions will find answers.

'I appreciate you' goes a long way.

Be a gentle man, with a gentle hand, and softly caress her broken.

With white, bloody knuckles, I finally opened up my hands and let it all go. Now, nothing remains except this longing, and I miss you.

Women fight for what they love, the things they care for. So if she stops fighting, you're getting dangerously close to losing her.

It took a little while for me to wisen up and take my own self by the hand, but I'm there now, loving myself for all that I am. This seems to be the part where I watch people come and go, and as painful as that may be, it is still necessary for my growth. And so, I carry on.

I lost myself in the
process of losing you, but
I gained a better me.

Fuck it! I'll hold myself..
love, listen to,
understand, validate,
respect, spend time on,
care for, trust, and
support my damn self.

I am tired. I'm so sick of contorting my soul to fit into this idea of what others want me to be. I am me. Take me as I am, or leave me the fuck alone.

Sure, it all falls to the ground, but then it is planted; it is watered and nurtured, and then, it blooms. Don't fight the natural ways of life; just allow all things to flow. The end of a thing is really just the beginning of another, after all.

Ink-stained hearts and paper souls, living in a world set on fire.

The best cure for
the aching of a
heart is to
strengthen those
muscles and
carry another
when their world
is falling apart.

Life is full of shitty things.
Learn to make fertilizer.

I can feel my
soul climbing up
in my throat and
trying to work
itself out of my
eyes again.

I've never done well with rejection. I pretend as if I'm fine and unbothered by it, but deep down inside the walls of my chest, my heart has stopped beating.

You find out who your friends are when you refuse to stuff yourself down into their box of expectations.

The universe keeps tossing it at me, and I can't tell if I've leveled up to the point of being at complete peace with everything or if I'm just numb?

The world
ended for me
many times,
and everyone
was so busy,
they failed to
even notice.

One thing I've learned in life is that the soul will never run out of tears.

And there are some days when I wish I could just run away with the wind.

I fall in love with kindness, nature, the sky, a cup of coffee, books, and anything else that doesn't take away from but adds peace to my wounded but still thriving soul.

The most beautiful thing to me is not the sunrise when the sky is in perfect hue, nor the flowers when sweetly in bloom; no, the most precious thing in the world to me are the way his eyes light up when he talks about the things he loves. That's when he shines at his brightest, when he's entirely himself, and that's when I love him the most.

Take me to that place where you saw me through the eyes of love, when all that I did made you fall so deep, and just hold me there.

Come, my love, sit
with me in between
the chaos and quiet
and find rest for
your wearied soul.
Come.

Oh, how I long to
feel your voice near,
the honey of your
hum, the whisper of
the earth in the
ocean of your lungs.

It was a perfectly imperfect love. Sometimes with sunrises, other times with storms, but always genuine in all things. From the smiles to the tears, they both did cry; it was a love that healed because it was real, and they actually tried.

Ever since you came into my life, I seem to have a garden growing in my heart. The weeds have begun to wilt, and the flowers seem to bloom brighter every day.

And when my world is crashing down around me, one look at you, and my heart smiles; everything else just kind of fades away.

She fell for him the same way the fire in the sky fell for the moon each night.

If I ever foolishly
forget to tell you that
I admire your smile or
that your hand is my
favorite one to hold,
then look back on
this, search your
heart, and remember.

As evening hit, I fell with great exhaustion into our bed, and you asked me how my day was. All I could think about was everything that pulled at my attention throughout the day: the dust, the screaming kiddos, the angry driver, and the lady who yelled at me at work- just all the issues that had left me worn. And just when I was about to unload all that mess, you smiled at me with those bright, sparkling eyes, and at that moment, it all just kind of faded away. "Fine, " I replied and returned your smile right back to you.

He made me laugh and smile but most importantly, he held my darkness, and I didn't know what else to do with that except for fall.
And that, I did..

Her heart will tell you everything you need to know if you'll but listen with yours.

Keep showing up for people. The world is in desperate need of souls who care. Be kind. Be gentle. Be caring. Be love in the flesh. You may be the only one who ever does.

In life, you will lose many people, but never the real ones.